SIGN

LINK

SIGN LANGUAGE LINK

A Pocket Dictionary
of Signs

CATH SMITH

Original illustrations by David Hodgson

CO-SIGN BOOKS UK

First published 1998 by Co-Sign Books UK,
c/o Alphabet Press, 70 Brunswick Street,
Stockton-on-Tees, TS18 1DW

ISBN   0-946252-33-5

Printed in Great Britain by
Alphabet Press,
70 Brunswick Street,
Stockton-on-Tees,
TS18 1DW
Telephone: 01642 895040

Dedicated to

Peter Paul Quinn and Norah Quinn

in loving memory and
gratitude

ACKNOWLEDGEMENTS

A special thank you to my family for their continued support and encouragement - my husband David, son William, sister Margaret, cousin Patricia, and Elsie and Ernest Smith my parents in-law, and to Beverley School for the Deaf for permission to use David Hodgson's illustrations in my previous books SIGNS MAKE SENSE, SIGN IN SIGHT and SIGN LANGUAGE COMPANION, a selection of which are used here in a completely new format.

To my Deaf co-workers Anita Duffy, Malcolm Haywood, Pauline Hodgson, Craig Jones and Sandra Teasdale for their tolerance at the constant requests of 'how do you sign ----- ?' and their generosity in sharing their native expertise with all those willing to learn - many many thanks.

CONTENTS

INTRODUCTION

Sign languages exist the world over wherever groups of Deaf* people come together, but although they are different languages, they share structures based on visual/spatial grammars that enable Deaf people from different countries to quickly establish common ground and understand each other.

British Sign Language (BSL) is the language of Britain's Deaf community, and in spite of regional variation (similar to dialect and accent in spoken language) it is used and understood by Deaf people throughout England, Wales, Scotland and Northern Ireland. It is even found on the other side of the world in Australia and New Zealand where it forms the basis of Auslan (Australian Sign Language). Early childhood deafness, with its profound effects on language and communication, is a shared experience, and Deaf people whose dominant language is BSL and **not English** represent the majority of Deaf community members.

---

* The convention of the upper case 'D' in *Deaf* refers to people who identify themselves as culturally Deaf sign language users.

However, the situation for most Deaf individuals is unusual compared to other language minority groups. For example, language is usually passed on from one generation to the next within families in a local community of language users. This rarely happens with BSL. The incidence of infant deafness is roughly one child in every thousand randomly distributed across the country, with the majority (90%) born to families who know nothing of deafness and are not themselves sign language users, at least in the early stages after diagnosis.

In addition, BSL was believed to deter deaf children's development of spoken language and was actively discouraged by deaf educationalists for over 100 years, an attitude still endorsed by many hearing professionals in spite of strong opposition from Deaf people. Deaf children **need** access to fluent and natural sign language users both within their own peer group, and through contact with adult sign language users - the Deaf role models who understand what it is like to be a deaf child in a hearing world.

Deaf people themselves greatly value their language and community with the whole shared experience of growing up deaf giving a totally different perspective on life, even to the extent that deafness itself is rarely seen as a problem. This can bring about the shared feeling of belonging and sense of closeness that leads Deaf people to seek each other out, and which can make people who aren't Deaf feel like outsiders.

Deaf people also live and work in the hearing world, and need and value their skills in English too. From their birth into a hearing family, to the birth of their own hearing children (90% of children born to Deaf couples are hearing), contact with the hearing world is inescapable and is handled with competence and confidence based on a lifetime's experience. It is hearing people who might feel inadequate, or suffer from culture shock when they encounter the Deaf world, driving greater and greater numbers to learn more about sign language.

This pocket book of sign language vocabulary is designed to assist such people, by providing an easily accessible form of reference for the numerous everyday situations in which Deaf and hearing people interface. To fulfil the most contant requests from Deaf people, it is packed with as much information on context and variation as possible within this convenient format. This gives a glimpse of the complexities of the language but the grammatical constructions of BSL require a visual way of thinking and of structuring thought that are outside the scope of a pocket dictionary (see SOURCES AND RECOMMENDED READING for further study).

The signs contained within are the building blocks of the language, capable of being inflected, modified and combined to express all the ideas, feelings and opinions that spoken language gives to those who are not Deaf. It is intended to give hearing people equal responsibilty for successful communication - sharing ideas and information in a way that is neither patronising nor condescending, but which offers equality and respect.

Even for those who have not yet had contact with Deaf people, BSL is a language worthy of study in its own right - a testament to the human mind's ability, when denied access to spoken language, to fulful its basic need and instinct for language construction - in an entirely different medium.

GUIDE TO HEADINGS AND CAPTIONS

Languages have very few direct word for word equivalents between each other, and the headings given for each sign are a guide to meaning rather than a direct translation. Where possible, more than one word heading is given, to give a clearer idea of its context.

The captions are intended to give extra information on the handshape, location and movement of signs, as well as additional details of variation, changes in context and details of facial and bodily expression when relevant and where space allows.

Signs and fingerspelling are described and illustrated as if the signer is right-handed, with the right hand always referred to as R. and the left hand as L.

Left-handed signers will use the reverse of this, with the left hand as dominant.

From the thumb, the fingers are referred to as index, middle, ring and little finger.

DIRECTION, ORIENTATION
AND MOVEMENT

Terms used to describe the direction in which the hands face, point or move are shown here. Description of hand orientation is based on the direction in which the palm faces regardless of whether the hand is open or closed.

As illustrated on the opposite page, the R. hand is palm left and the L. hand is palm right, or they can also be described as palm facing.

The hand may be described as 'pointing' up, forward etc., even if the fingers are bent in a different direction or closed.

As illustrated, both hands are pointing forward, thumbs up.

Diagonal movements are described 'forward/left' or 'back/right' and so on.

Some signs start with a full description of handshape and position before movement is made. This is then called a **formation**, which means they keep their position together as they move.

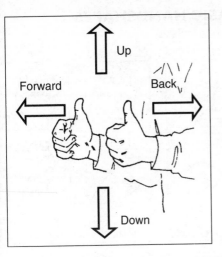

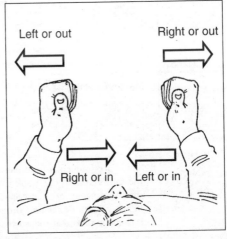

BASIC HANDSHAPES

Closed Hand

Flat Hand

Clawed Hand

Fist

Bent Hand

Bunched hand

'C' Hand

'M' Hand

Full 'C' Hand

Full 'O' Hand

'L' Hand

Cupped Hand

'N' Hand

'Y' Hand

'O' Hand

Open Hand

'V' Hand

These are frequently used handshapes in BSL and the terms used in this book to describe them. If the handshapes are described for example as *index, middle finger and thumb extended*, then it is understood that the other fingers are closed.

16

ARROWS

Repeated movement

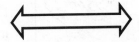

Movement in one direction
then the other

Movement ends with
stress

Hands move apart

Open hand closes

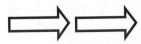

A broken movement

Closed hand opens

Very small repeated movements

Impact on point drawn

Hands drawn in dotted
lines show the **start** of
the sign. Hands drawn
in solid lines show the
finish.

17

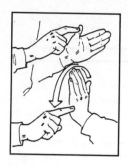

ABOUT, CONCERNING

Fingerspell 'A', then R. index sweeps around L. fingertips to form 'T', or edge of R. fist, index extended, makes circles on L. palm. Varies.

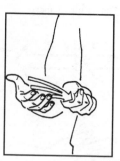

ACCEPT, GET, RECEIVE

Palm up open hand moves back to body closing to a fist. Both hands may be used.

ACCESS, THROUGH

R. flat hand moves foward/left through the fingers of L. hand. Also means **interfere, interrupt, butt in.** Directional.

ACCIDENT

Hands form fingerspelt 'A', then R. hand forms 'C' and moves right in two small hops, or palm left R clawed hand shakes back and forth at side of head. Shoulders lift. May vary.

ACCUSE, BLAME

Indexes point and move forward/right, or in direction of person referred to. Eyes are narrowed and brows furrowed.

ADVANTAGE, BENEFIT, GAIN

R. 'O' hand starts palm up then twists up and over to palm down, so that index and thumb tips brush down side of chest. Also means *profit*.

19

AEROPLANE, FLIGHT

R. closed hand with thumb and little finger extended, moves forward/up at head height. May move down onto L. palm (*airport, landing*).

AFTER, LATER

Extended index twists left to right in small arc (may repeat), or extended thumb twists from palm down to palm up (forward or right). Varies.

AFTERNOON

Tips of 'N' hand touch chin, then twist to point forward, or brush forward against tips of L. 'N' hand (regional).

AGAIN, OFTEN, REPEAT

Palm left R. 'V' hand shakes forward/down twice. Also means *frequently*.

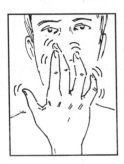

AGE, AGED, HOW OLD?

Fingers of palm back open hand flutter in front of nose. Eyebrows are raised or furrowed for question form in *how old?*

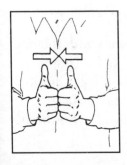

AGREE, SUIT, APPROPRIATE

Closed hands with thumbs up move in towards each other so that knuckles touch. The head nods and lips are pressed together.

21

ALARM (e.g. fire), BELL

Edge of palm forward R. index bangs against L. palm several times. Also means *alarm clock, bell ring.*

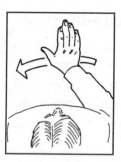

ALL, EVERYONE

Palm down flat hand makes horizontal sweep in front of body.

ALL RIGHT, FINE, OK

Closed hands with thumbs extended and slightly pointing out, make small outward circles (also regional sign for *finished*). May vary.

22

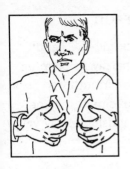

ANGRY, FRUSTRATED, MAD

Clawed hands move sharply up body twisting to palm up (also **temper**), can be one hand, or alternate movement. Brows are furrowed, cheeks puffed.

ANIMAL, CREATURE

Palm down clawed hands make alternate forward circular clawing movements.

ANSWER, REPLY

Tip of R. index makes repeated contact with L. thumb tip in backward brushing movement. L. hand may be closed with thumb up.

23

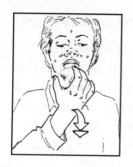

APPLE, FRUIT

Palm back full 'C' hand twists sharply to palm up twice near mouth. A single movement may be used. Handshape may vary slightly.

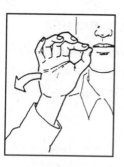

ASK, REQUEST

R. 'O' hand moves forward from side of mouth in small arc, or palm forward bent hand makes short repeated forward movement. Directional.

ATTITUDE

Palm back flat hand moves forward from in front of face, twisting to palm forward.

AWAKE, AWARE/NESS

Index fingers and thumbs flick open at sides of eyes. One hand can be used. Also means *wake up.*

BABY, INFANT, DOLL

Arms move from side to side in rocking movement.

BAD, TERRIBLE, SERIOUS

Little finger held up with small movement (can be forward, back or side to side). Face and body indicate negative form. Both hands can be used.

25

BANANA

Hands move in action of holding and peeling banana. Can be outline of shape with thumbs and index fingers.

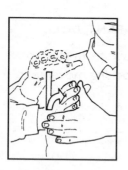

BECAUSE

L. flat hand held with thumb up. R. flat hand contacts edge of L. index, then inside of L. thumb.

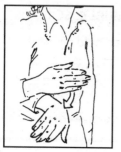

BEEN, DONE

Flat hand flips over to palm down in quick movement. Also means *from, where from?* Eyebrows raised for question form.

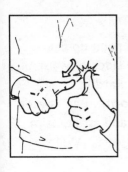

BEST

R. thumb strikes tip of L. thumb in sharp forward movement

BETTER

R. thumb tip brushes forward twice against tip of L. thumb tip.

BIRD, BEAK

Index finger and thumb open and close in front of mouth.

BIRTHDAY

Blades of palm up flat hands on sides of waist move forward/in (**birth, born**), then sweep upwards and apart, palm back. Regional. Will vary.

BISCUIT

Fingertips of R. clawed hand tap twice near left elbow. May vary regionally.

BLUE

R. flat hand makes small circular movement on L. palm or wrist. Can be made on back of palm down L. hand. Colours vary regionally.

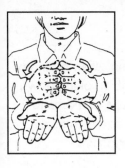

BOOK, CATALOGUE

Flat hands held together palm to palm twist open to palm up. Movement may be repeated

BOOK, BOOKING, RESERVE

Closed hands contact at second knuckles. Also means *appointment*. Can be R. flat hand flipping over to palm down on L. palm, or other variation.

BORE/D, BORING, DULL

R. hand taps mouth several times in action of stifling a yawn, with appropriate facial/bodily expression, and open mouth.

BOY

R. index brushes left across chin. Can be index and thumb stroking down chin, or tips of 'N' hand brushing down chin. Varies regionally.

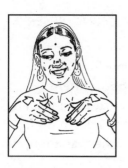

BREAK, REST, RELAX

Thumb tips of palm down hands contact upper chest, head may be tilted to one side. Can be one hand only.

BRITAIN, BRITISH

Palm down open hands make small repeated movement down, or palm back closed hands contact chest twice (regional).

BROTHER

Closed hands with thumbs up rub knuckles against each other.

BUS, MINIBUS

Closed hands (can be palm up) move in steering action, then thumb moves forward, or palm left R. bent 'V' hand moves slightly forward (regional).

CAKE, SCONE

Tips of R. clawed hand tap back of L. hand. Movement can be repeated.

CAN, ABLE, POSSIBLE

'C' hand pointing back in front of nose moves forward/down as index flexes. May repeat. Can be located on the forehead.

CANCEL, CALL OFF

R. index draws a cross on L. palm. Can be palm down flat hands which start crossed and move sharply apart.

CAN'T, UNABLE

Index moves down and loops over in the form of an X, accompanied by head shake. May start from forehead. Both hands can be used.

CAR PARK

Sign for **car**, then blade of R. flat hand contacts L. palm several times, moving to the right.

CAREFUL, CAREFULLY

Indexes held under eyes; index fingers flex as hands move forward/down. Also means **be careful, take care**.

CAT

Fingers flex as hands move out from sides of mouth to indicate whiskers. Can be R. hand stroking back of L. closed hand (regional).

CELEBRATE, HAVE FUN

Palm in 'Y' hands move in towards each other, up, and out again whilst rotating from wrists, cheeks puffed. Also means *party, social*.

CHANGE, ALTER

Indexes extended with hands facing and in contact, twist to change positions. One of a number of variations.

CHEAT, TWIST

Fists held together twist against each other, eyes narrowed, or thumb tip moves down cheek (hand is closed, thumb out), also meaning *sly, crafty*.

CHECK, INSPECT

Two 'Y' hands move down with quick twisting movements from wrists.
One hand may be used.
Directional.

CHEEK/Y, INSULT, BARE

Bent index and thumb grasp cheek with slight shaking movement.

CHEQUE, SLIP, TICKET

Index fingers and thumbs move apart in outline shape, size may vary. 'Y' hands can be used.

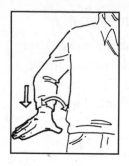

CHILDREN

Palm down flat hand makes small downward repeated movement a few inches apart (single movement for *child*). Two hands may be used, moving apart.

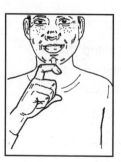

CHOCOLATE

Index edge of R. 'C' hand taps against the chin twice. Also one version of *jealous*. Varies regionally.

CHRISTMAS

Tips of R. hand brush backwards against back of L. hand, then R. hand closes and moves down onto back of L. One of several variations.

CLASS, CLASSROOM

'C' hands touch at finger-tips then swivel in forward arc to finish with blades touching.   One of several variations.

CLEAN, CLEAR

R. flat hand sweeps forward along palm up L. hand.

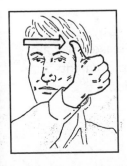

CLEVER, BRIGHT

Thumb tip moves across forehead in sharp movement.

37

COACH

Full 'C' hands held facing each other pull diagonally apart, L. forward/left and R. backward/right.

COFFEE

'C' hand makes small quick twisting movements near mouth. Can be edge of R. fist on top of L. fist making circular grinding movements.

COKE, COLA

'C' hand makes two short forward movements from side to side.

COLD, CHILLY, WINTER

Closed hands move in and out slightly towards each other, or elbows pull into body in shivering action. Cheeks may be puffed.

COLLEGE

'C' hand makes small quick twisting movements at temple. One of several regional signs.

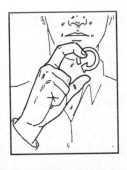

COLOUR

Palm left R. 'C' hand makes small circles near chin, or palm forward open hand makes small vertical circles, or other regional variations.

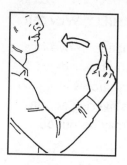

COME, COME BACK

Extended index moves back towards body (index may be bent). Index flexes several times for **come here.** Directional.

COMMUNICATE

'C' hands move alternately backwards and forwards. Full 'C' hands or palm up flat hands may also be used.

COMPLAIN, GRUMBLE

Palm up clawed hand brushes up chest twice. Face and body show negative feeling.

COMPUTER

'C' hands make vertical circles simultaneously, or fingers of palm down open hands wiggle, also meaning *keyboard, key in, type*.

CONFIDENT

Index edge of R. 'C' hand taps chest twice. A movement up or down means *gain confidence*, or *lose confidence,* respectively.

CONTACT, CONNECT

Hands move towards each other and fingers of 'O' hands interlock. Directional. Also means *link, join*.

CONTINUE, CARRY ON, STILL

Palm down 'C' hands move right, or forward (may repeat). Can be one hand. Short downward movement gives *stay, remain, be still.*

COURSE, SCHEME

R. 'C' hand moves down along left forearm, or along L. extended index.

DAILY, EVERY DAY

The backs of the fingers brush forwards across the cheek. Can be repeated contact of index against side of chin.

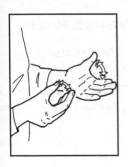

DAMP, MOIST, WET

Fingers held straight; hands open and close onto thumbs, twice. One hand may be used

DANCE, DANCING

'V' hands make downward flicking movements from wrists as hands move from side to side. 'N' hands may be used, or other variation.

DANGER, DANGEROUS

Palm left R. flat hand moves sharply up to contact forehead. May be repeated. Also means *risk, risky.*

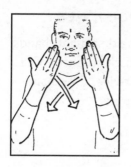

DARK, EVENING, NIGHT

Palm back flat hands swing in/down to cross each other. One of several variations for *evening, night.*

DATE

Palm left R. closed hand taps side of chin twice. May tap front of chin, also meaning *number.*

DAUGHTER, DAD, DADDY

Hands form quick repeated fingerspelt 'D' formation.

DAY, LIGHT

Palm back flat hands start crossed and swing upwards and apart from the elbows. *Day* is often fingerspelt.

DEAD, DEATH, DIE

Palm facing 'N' hands twist down sharply from wrists to point forward. If movement is slow, the meaning is *dying*.

DEAF, DEAF PERSON

Tips of 'N' hand contact ear. Cheeks may be puffed, meaning *profoundly deaf, really deaf*.

DEAF CLUB

Tips of 'N' hand contact ear, then hand moves out slightly as fingers bend into 'C' shape. Regional. *Club* often fingerspelt contraction.

DIFFERENT

Indexes held together, palm down move apart twisting to palm up.

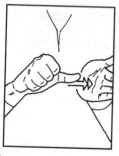

DIFFICULT/Y, PROBLEM

R. thumb tip taps centre of L. palm twice. Also means *hard*.

DINNER, MEAL

Palm back 'N' hands move
alternately up to mouth.
Can be two 'N' hands edge
to edge making small
sawing movement.

DIRT/Y, GRIMY

Palms of open hands rub
from side to side against
each other (can be circular
movement), with
appropriate facial
expression.

DISABLED, DISABILITY

Hands form fingerspelt 'D',
then R. index moves down
along fingertips of L. open
hand. One of several
variations.

DISAGREE

Closed hands contact each other, then spring open and apart accompanied by head shake.

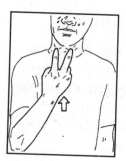

DISAPPOIN/TED

Tips of 'V' hand prod into neck. Also a regional sign for *miss* (lips pressed together).

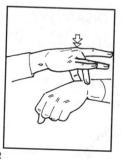

DOCTOR

R. middle finger and thumb tips tap L. wrist twice. Index and thumb tips can be used, or tips of 'O' hand move side to side on chest (*medical*).

DOG

'N' hands pointing down make small movements down. Also back of bent hand under chin, or flat hand tapping thigh (regional).

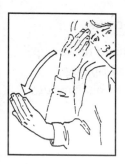

DON'T KNOW

Tips of flat hand contact forehead, then hand drops forward/down accompanied by head shake and shrugged shoulders.

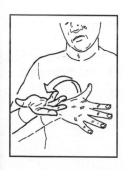

DON'T LIKE

Open hand on chest moves forward, twisting to palm up with negative expression.

DON'T UNDERSTAND

Index fingers flick backwards at sides of head, with lip pattern 'Pow!' or 'Whoosh!' Regional. Also means *over my head*.

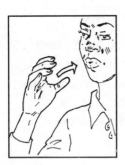

DRINK, GLASS

Full 'C' hand moves up with small tipping movement near mouth.

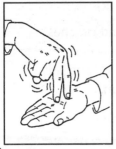

DRUNK, TIPSY

R. 'V' hand (legs classifier) stands on L. palm, fingers bend as hand rotates slightly.

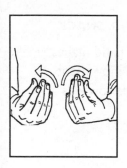

DRY, DRIED

The thumbs rub across the pads of the fingers. One hand may be used.

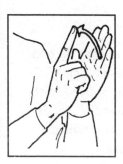

EARLY, EARLIER

Upright R. index makes small backward movement on L. palm. One of several variations.

EASY, SIMPLE, SOFT

Index finger prods the cheek twice. Cheeks may be puffed out meaning *dead easy, doddle.*

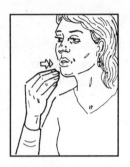

EAT, FOOD, SNACK

Bunched hand makes small repeated movement backwards towards mouth.

EGG

R. 'N' hand (can be bent index) makes slicing movement above L. fist. Can be bent 'V' hands touching then twisting down/apart.

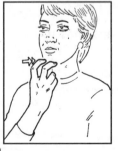

ELECTRIC/ITY, BATTERY

Tips of R. bent 'V' hand tap chin twice. *Electricity* can also be signed with palm forward index moving down in sharp zig-zag.

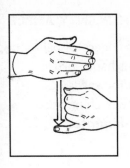

END, FINAL, LAST

Palm back R. flat hand moves down onto extended L. little finger. R. hand can also be palm down or palm up.

ENGLAND, ENGLISH

R. extended index makes small repeated rubbing movement forward/back along L. extended index.

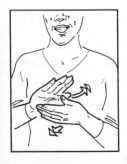

ENJOY, HAPPY, PLEASURE

Flat hands brush against each other in repeated movement.

53

ENOUGH, PLENTY, AMPLE

Backs of fingers of palm back bent hand brush upwards/forwards twice under chin. Also means *adequate*.

EQUIPMENT, MACHINE

Palm back clawed hands swivel towards each other from wrists so that fingers interlink. Also means *engineering, technology*.

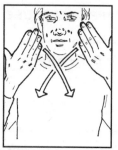

EVENING, DARK, NIGHT

Palm back flat hands pointing up, swing down/in to cross each other. One of several variations.

EXAM, TEST

Index edge of R. 'N' hand makes short repeated forward movement on L. palm. One of several variations.

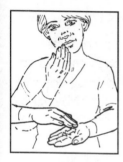

EXCUSE, PARDON ME

Fingertips touch mouth then L. palm with small rubbing movement (if circular, can mean *apologise, forgive*) Fingerspelt 'EX' also used.

EXPECT, TAKE CARE

Indexes held under eyes, move forward and flex, (regional). Can be thumb of closed hand moving back to tap chest twice for *expect, intend.*

55

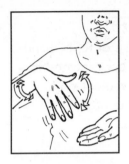

EXPENSIVE, DEAR

Tips of R. open hand hit L. palm, then R. hand moves to the right shaking from wrist. The cheeks may be puffed.

EXPERIENCE/D

R. thumb tip contacts forehead, then changes to flat hand brushing down across L. palm. May vary.

EXPLAIN, TELL ABOUT

Index moves from mouth then hands rotate round each other in circular movements. Directional. Also means *relate, story*.

FALL, FALL OVER

R. 'V' hand (legs classifier) stands on L. palm then twists over to palm up. Handshape and movement may change in context.

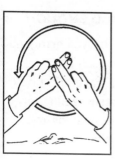

FAMILY

Fingerspelt 'F' formation moves in small horizontal circle. Can be palm down open hand in same movement.

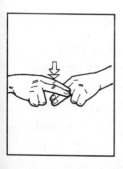

FATHER, DAD, DADDY

Fingers of fingerspelt 'F' formation tap together twice. Also mean *Friday* in some regions.

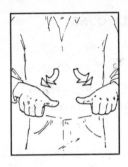

FAVOURITE, PREFER/ENCE

Closed hands with thumbs extended make two small downward movements. One of several variations.

FED UP, HAD ENOUGH

Bent hand moves firmly up under chin (can be repeated). Face and body show negative feeling, or can change meaning to *full, I'm full.*

FEEL, EMOTION, SENSE

Tips of middle fingers brush upwards on body (open hands may be used). May be repeated. One hand may be used.

FILL IN (form), NOTE DOWN

R. 'N' hand makes several
short forward movements
as it moves down behind
L. flat hand.   R. bent 'V'
hand may be used.

FINGERSPELL, SPELL

Finger and thumb tips of
bunched hands contact
with fingers wiggling as
formation moves right (for
British two-handed
system).

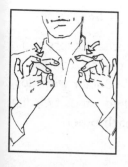

FINISH, COMPLETE

Middle fingers and thumb
tips make quick repeated
contact. Regional. One
hand may be used. One of
several variations.

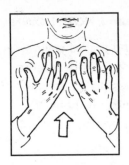

FIRE, BURN, FLAMES

Palm back hands move upwards with fingers wiggling. Can be palm facing, moving up and down alternately. May vary in context.

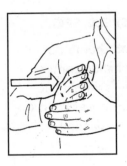

FIRST, INITIAL

R. hand strikes inside of L. thumb. Can be palm forward index twisting sharply to palm back, or several other regional signs.

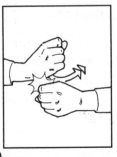

FIX, MEND, REPAIR

R. fist brushes across top of L. fist twice. Can be repeated contact with tips of bunched hands twisting against each other.

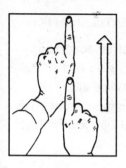

FOLLOW, GO ALONG WITH

Indexes point and move forward R. behind L. Indexes can be upright (person classifiers), and also mean *work shadow*.

FOLLOW, TAIL, TAIL-GATE

Flat hands (vehicle classifiers) point and move forward, R. behind L. Movement may vary in context.

FORGET, FORGETFUL

Tips of full 'O' hand touch forehead then hand springs open in short forward movement. One of several variations.

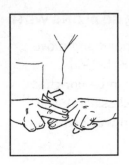

FREE, GRATIS, BLANK

Fingerspelt 'F' formation;
R. hand fingers brush
forward twice along L.
A circular movement gives
a regional sign for **Friday.**

FRIEND, MATE, PAL

R. hand clasps L. in short
shaking movement, or
closed hands, thumbs up,
bang together or twist
against each other
(regional).

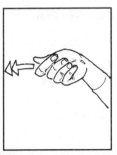

FRY, FRY UP, FRYING PAN

Thumb tucked into bent
index; hand makes small
forward shaking
movements. Can be palm
in 'V' hands twisting from
the wrists.

FUNNY, LAUGH

Bent index and thumb shake slightly from side to side near chin. Two hands can be used in alternate movement, L. under R.

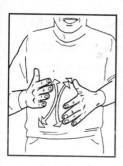

GAME, PLAY

Open hands brush alternately up and down against each other twice. Can be fingerspelt 'G' formation, or other variation.

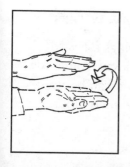

GARDEN/ER, DIG,

Flat hand turns over from palm up to palm down in small repeated forward movement. One of several variations.

GIRL, LASS

Index makes small strokes forward twice on cheek (or across chin). Can be index pointing left, moving to right on brow (regional).

GIVE, HAND OVER, PASS

Hands move forward together (can be one hand). Handshape and direction may change in context. Also means *gift, offer, present*.

GO, GO AWAY, SEND

Index swings forward, pointing away from body. A flat hand can be used. Will vary in context.

GOD, BOSS, CHIEF, HEAD

Index pointing up above head, moves forward slightly with stress, or can be small upward twist from wrist. Both hands for **authority**.

GOOD, GREAT, HELLO

Extended thumb makes small movement forward, both hands may be used. With raised eyebrows also means **all right?**

GOODBYE, BYE, CHEERIO

Hand bends at palm knuckles in repeated movement, or shakes slightly from side to side.

GOOD LUCK, LUCK, LUCKY

Index and thumb extended, tip of thumb contacts nose, then hand twists sharply forward to palm down. One of several variations.

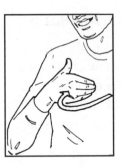

GOOD-MORNING, MORNING

Tips of R. bent hand, thumb up, touch left, then right upper chest. Can be two bent hands, or closed hands, moving up chest (regional).

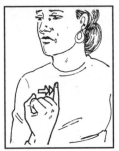

GUILT/Y, MY FAULT

Edge of extended little finger taps chest twice. A circular movement gives a regional sign for *sorry, apologise.*

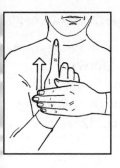

HAPPEN, CROP UP, OCCUR

R. index moves up sharply behind L. hand, or index flicks upwards in front of L. hand (emphatically for **sudden, suddenly**).

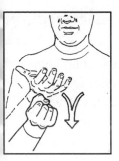

HAVE, GET, POSSESS

Palm up clawed hand moves down slightly, closing sharply to a fist.

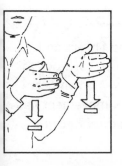

HAVE TO, COMPULSORY

Flat hands held apart with palms facing move down sharply with emphasis. Also means **must, obliged to**.

67

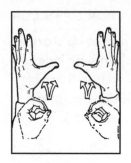

HEADLIGHTS, HEADLAMPS

Full 'O' hands spring open with slight forward movement. Repeated movement gives *flashing headlights*. Directional.

HEARING, HEARING PERSON

Tip of index finger contacts ear then chin (may tap chin twice). Sometimes made with extended thumb.

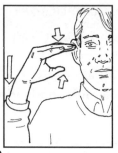

HEARING LOSS, DEAFENED

Bent hand fingers and thumb close together as hand moves down near ear. Slow movement indicates *gradual hearing loss.*

HELLO

Palm forward open hand moves to right in small arc. Hand may twist right at wrist closing to thumb up palm left, or other variation.

HELP, AID, ASSIST

Edge of R. closed hand rests on L. palm and formation moves forward or back, or in direction appropriate to context (directional).

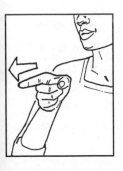

HER, HE, HIM, IT, SHE

Index indicates person/thing referred to, accompanied by eye gaze. A sideways sweep indicates plural. Directional.

69

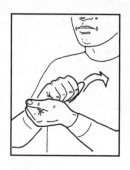

HIRE, BORROW, LEND

Closed hands, one on top of the other, move back to body in small arc (or forward, according to context). Directional.

HOPE, WISH

Crossed fingers make slight forward movement (can be one hand), or palm left R. full 'C' closes sharply near mouth (regional).

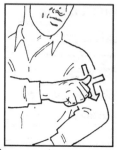

HOSPITAL, FIRST AID

R. thumb tip (can be index tip) draws small cross on left upper arm. One of many variations. Also means *ambulance, nurse.*

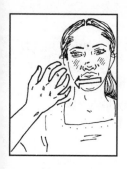

HOT, HEAT

R. clawed hand moves sharply left to right in front of mouth. Can be flat hand drawn across forehead, then shaking downwards.

HOTEL, LODGE, STAY OVER

Flat hands (can be one hand) move down from sides of head, twisting to palm down. Also means *accommodation, residential.*

HOUSE, HOME

Tips of 'N' hands contact at an angle, then move apart/down in outline of building. Flat hands can be used.

71

HOW?

Knuckles of clawed hands tap together twice. Can be palm back or palm up. Face/body indicate question form.

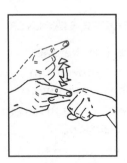

HURRY UP, QUICKLY

R. index taps on L. several times very quickly. With appropriate facial/bodily expression, also means *emergency, urgent.*

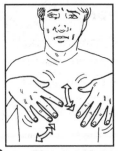

HURT, PAINFUL, SORE

Open hands shake up and down alternately. Can be one hand. Face/body indicate negative form. Also means *injure, suffer.*

HUSBAND, WIFE, SPOUSE

R. thumb and index (or thumb and middle finger) make repeated contact with upper L. ring finger. Also means *wedding, ring.*

I, ME

Index fingertip touches chest.

IDEA, NOTION

Index contacts forehead, then moves out and bends with thumb up, or index flexed on thumb flicks up off forehead (also means *understand*).

73

IGNORE, TAKE NO NOTICE

Hands with indexes extended (can be one hand only), flick sharply down/sideways from near ears. May change direction in context.

ILL/NESS, SICK, UNWELL

Edges of little fingers (can be one hand only) make short movement down chest. Can be R index moving down from forehead onto L. index.

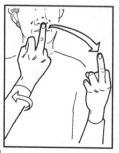

IMITATION, FAKE, MOCK

Tip of R. middle finger touches nose, twists and moves forward, then taps the L. middle fingertip twice. Also means *false, pretend.*

IMPORTANT, TOP

Palm of R. hand contacts tip of L. index, (may tap twice). R. hand may spring open from full 'O' as it comes down onto L. index.

IMPROVE, IMPROVEMENT

Index and thumb tip of R. 'O' hand move upwards along L. extended index.

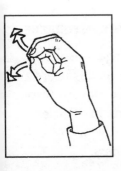

INDICATOR (vehicle)

Fingers of full 'O' hand make small repeated opening movements. Directional.

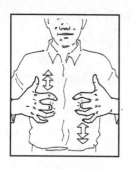

INTEREST/ED, KEEN

Fingers clawed, tips of middle fingers rub in alternate small quick up/down movements on chest. Also means *enthusiasm, stimulate*.

INTERPRET, INTERPRETER

'N' hands make repeated alternate twisting movements forward/backwards from wrists. 'V' hands sometimes used.

INTERRUPT, INTERFERE

R. hand fingers prod through L. hand fingers twice. Directional. Also means *butt in.* Single forward movement means *access.*

JOKE, KID, HAVE ON

Thumb tip of 'V' hand brushes tip of nose twice, or palm down R. 'V' hand (or open hand) brushes forward twice along L. extended index.

KEEN, ENTHUSIASTIC

Tips of clawed hands make alternate short rubbing movements on the chest, with appropriate expression. Also means *eager, interest.*

KISS, PECK

Tips of R. 'N' hand touch lips, then twist to palm down and contact tips of L. 'N' hand (will vary in context). One of several variations.

KITCHEN

Middle knuckle of R. bent index taps middle of L. extended index twice (repeated fingerspelt 'K').

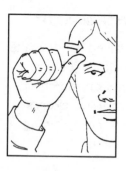

KNOW, KNOWLEDGE

Tip of extended thumb contacts forehead. Contact may be repeated. A forward flick of the thumb gives **understand** (regional).

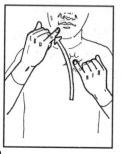

LAST, WORST

R. little finger strikes tip of L. in upward (can be downward) movement. Can be R. flat hand brought down onto L. little finger (**last, end**).

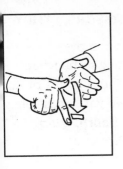

LATE, OVERDUE

Tip of R. thumb maintains contact with L. palm as index swivels sharply forward/down. May be index only, with thumb tucked in.

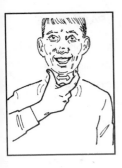

LAUGH/TER, FUNNY

'C' hand makes small side to side shaking movements near chin. Two hands can be used in small alternate movement, L. under R.

LAZY, IDLE

R. hand taps left elbow twice (R. clawed hand gives *biscuit*), or palm back closed hands, middle fingers up, move down twice.

LEARN, ABSORB, STUDY

Open hand moves back to head closing to bunched hand, or index edges of R. palm down flat hands rub together (*learn, train, practice*).

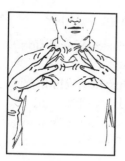

LEISURE, SPARE TIME

Thumb tips of open hands contact chest as finger wiggle (can be one hand only). Also means *holiday, break, relaxation*.

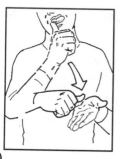

LETTER, MAIL

R. thumb tip touches mouth, then moves down to touch L. palm. In some regions also means *stamp, insurance*.

LIE, LIAR, FIB, UNTRUTH

Edge of R. index pointing left rubs across chin sharply to the right. Is also one version of *Russia, Russian*.

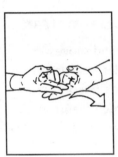

LIFT, RIDE, TRANSPORT

Palm up 'N' hands, R. on L., formation moves forward, meaning *give a lift/ride to, transport* in a car etc.

LIGHT-FLASHING DOORBELL

Thumb makes short movement forward, then hand moves up as fingers spring open, twice. (This is an alerting device available to deaf people).

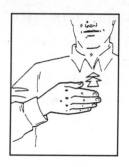

LIKE, APPROVE, ENJOY

Hand taps chest twice (also means *fond of*). Open hand on chest moves forward, and closes with index up to give *if you like, please yourself.*

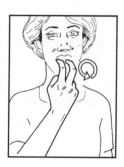

LIPREAD, LIP- PATTERN

Bent 'V' hand moves in small circles near mouth. Also means *lipspeaker, oral.* Directional (can be palm forward, held forward).

LIVE, LIFE, ALIVE

Tip of middle finger rubs up and down on chest. A clawed hand may be used. Also means *address* and is a regional sign for *toilet.*

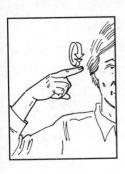

LONDON, NOISE, NOISY

Index makes forward circles, pointing towards ear. Palm down bent hands, make two small movements down for *London, shopping* (regional).

LONELY, ISOLATED

R. index moves down behind L. hand then both hands open and swing to point down. First part of sign also means *alone, individual, only.*

LOOK, SEE, WATCH

'V' hand moves forward from near eye, or will be located and directed with movement appropriate to context (fingers represent direction of eye gaze).

LOOP SYSTEM

Palm facing 'O' hands move apart in forward arcs. Sign can be made on the body to refer to personal loop worn round the neck. (Listening device for hearing aid users).

LOSE, LOST, DROP

Palm down full 'O' hands move down/apart, springing open. If the sign is made palm up, the meaning is *waste, wasted.*

LOTTERY (national lottery)

Hand is held palm forward, with index and middle fingers crossed and thumb extended.

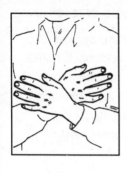

LOVE, AFFECTION

Crossed over hands on chest. For **love, adore, fond of**, palm back flat hands touch chest, then close in forward movement palm down, thumbs extended.

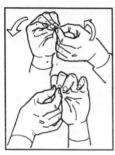

MAKE, CREATE, FIX

Tips of bunched hands twist against each other, twice, (if hands also move up, meaning is **construct**). Can be R. fist striking top of L.

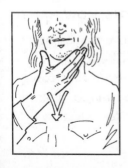

MAN, MALE, MASCULINE

Hand strokes chin as fingers close onto thumb, may be repeated, or palm left R. full 'C' hand moves forward from chin closing to a fist.

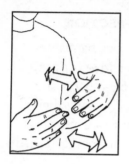

MANAGE, SORT OUT, ARRANGE

Fingers brush against each other as palm back hands move alternately backwards and forwards. Also means *anyway, organise, never mind*.

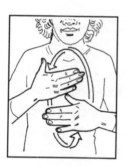

MANNER/S, BEHAVIOUR

Flat hands brush alternately backwards down body. With head tilted and lips pressed together, means *calm, patient, tolerant.*

MANY, LOTS, HOW MANY?

Hands move apart, fingers wiggling. Cheeks may be puffed. Also means *too many, too much*. Raised eyebrows for question form.

MAYBE, MIGHT, POSSIBLY

'Y' hand twists quickly from wrist. Lips may be stretched. Can be palm up flat hands moving up and down alternately (also *doubt, uncertain*).

MEAN, MEANING

Fingers of R. flat hand make small circular movements on L. palm. Also means *context, explanation, story*.

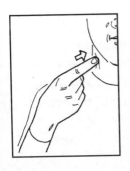

MEAT, BEEF, BUTCHER

Index prods into neck (may repeat), or bent index and thumb grasp cheek (also meaning *bare, flesh, insult*). As shown, also means *kill*.

MEET, FACE TO FACE

Extended indexes (person classifiers) move towards each other, located and directed to suit context. Without movement, meaning is **one to one**.

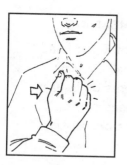

MINE, MY, BELONG TO ME

Palm back closed hand touches chest. Can be repeated movement. Also means **belonging to me, my own.**

MINICOM, TEXT 'PHONE

L. 'Y' hand, palm down/back, above wiggling fingers of R. palm down clawed hand. Formation moves forward or back for **call by minicom.**

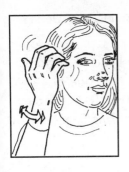

MISTAKE, ACCIDENT, SORRY

Clawed hand at side of
head, shakes back and
forth, or side to side in
front of head (palm back),
or other variation.
Shoulders lift.

MONEY, CASH, FINANCE

R. thumb tucked into bent
index, taps L. palm twice.
R. handshape may vary.
Can be thumb of full 'C'
hand on L. palm (*funds*).

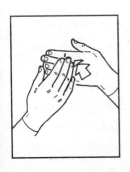

MORE

Palm back flat hands (L.
hand can be closed). R.
taps back of L. twice, or
hands start in contact,
then R. moves forward
(also meaning *further*).

MOTHER, MUM, MUMMY

R. 'M' hand taps twice on L. palm. In some regions, 'M' hand taps side of forehead, or R. index taps back of L. ring finger twice.

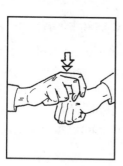

NORTHEN IRELAND, IRISH

Tips of R. bent 'V' hand tap back of L. closed hand twice. Also one version of *potato*.

NAME, CALL, CALLED

'N' hand on side of forehead, moves and twists forward, or palm facing 'V' hands move slightly outwards as fingers flex (*called, entitled*).

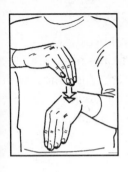

NAUGHTY, BOTHER

Tips of R. bent hand tap back of L. hand (or forearm) twice. Also means *nuisance, trouble.* One of several variations.

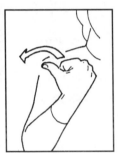

NEIGHBOUR, NEXT

Closed hand with thumb extended twists from palm down to palm up. Directional (can be a forward movement, or other in context).

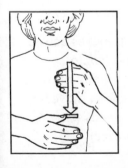

NEVER

Palm back hands (L. hand can be closed or bent), R. flat hand brushes sharply down back of L. hand.

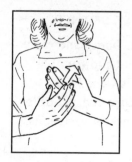

NEW, MODERN

R. flat hand brushes up back (or front) of L. Can be repeated. Also means *fashion* and *fresh* (R. hand fingers may open).

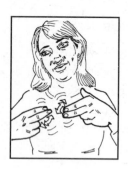

NEWS

Tips of 'N' hands brush against each other in repeated alternate forward and backward movement.

NICE, SWEET, TASTY

Thumb tip moves across chin, (also *delicious, lovely*), or index of R. 'L' hand on cheek moves right and bends (also *lovely, pretty*).

NO, DENY, REFUSE

Palm back closed hand twists sharply to palm forward, (accompanied by head shake). Can also mean *turn away* (the head turns sharply).

NOISY, LOUD, SOUND

Index moves in forward circular movements at side of head. Also means *London*.

NOT SURE, UNCERTAIN

R. flat hand, edge down on L. palm, wavers slightly side to side (lips pressed together). Also means *doubtful, hesitant, unsure.*

NOT YET, BEFORE

Closed hands, palm forward/down, shake in small quick side to side movements. Also means *wait* (or two small downward movements).

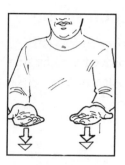

NOW, PRESENT, TODAY

Palm up flat hands make short downward movement, twice. One sharp movement gives *at once, right now, immediately*.

NURSERY

Tip of extended middle finger taps chin twice (regional). One of several variations.

OFFICE

Palm forward 'O' hand makes small circles (regional), or moves right, palm down, with small up/down movements, or other variation.

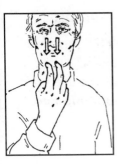

OLD, AGED, ELDERLY

Palm back 'V' hand (or bent 'V'), moves down in front of nose as fingers flex, or hand bends backwards. Also means *dark, night* (regional).

ORANGE

Palm forward (or palm left), clawed hand opens and closes at side of mouth, or fingers may flex. Refers to the colour, fruit or drink.

PANIC, FRANTIC

Open hands move alternately forward/down several times. The head twists from side to side and the mouth is open.

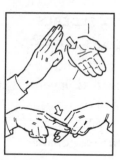

PARENT, PARENTS

Fingerspelt 'M' formation followed by fingerspelt 'F'. Also means *mother and father, mum and dad.*

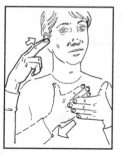

PARTIALLY DEAF

Edge of R. flat hand moves back/right across L. palm, (also means *half, part*) followed by tips of 'N' hand touching ear (*deaf*).

PAY, PAYMENT

R. hand moves forward off L. palm (directional). Repeated for **regular payment, rent**. R. h/shape may vary e.g. 'O' hand, full 'C', or bunched hand.

PEOPLE, HUMAN, PUBLIC

Index and thumb stroke chin, then index brushes forward on cheek, or palm forward index moves down in sharp zig-zag, or other variations.

PET, CAT, STROKE

R. hand strokes down back of L. closed hand, twice. Regional.

PICK, CHOOSE, SELECT

Index closes onto thumb in short backward movement. Can be both both hands alternately, also meaning *raffle*. Directional.

PILL, TABLET

R. index and thumb flick open, twice, near mouth. R. hand may start in contact with L. palm, before moving to mouth.

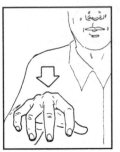

PLACE, TOWN, COUNTRY

Clawed hand makes short movement down (can be above upright L. index). May make small circular movement (open hand may also be used).

PLAN, DESIGN, STRATEGY

Tips of R. 'V' hand contact L. palm, twice, as R. hand twists from palm back to palm down. Located on forehead means *translate, work out, change of mind.*

PLAY, GAME

Open hands make simultaneous circular movements, upwards/ apart, or brush palm to palm, up and down against each other.

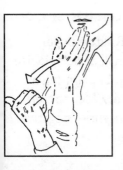

PLEASE, IF YOU PLEASE

Tips of flat hand touch mouth, then hand moves forward/down as fingers close onto palm. Can be made without final closing movement.

PLEASED, APPRECIATE

Flat hand rubs in circles on chest, or hands brush together twice, palm to palm (also *enjoy, glad, happy*). Face/body show positive expression.

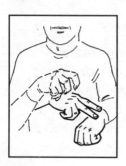

POLICE, POLICE OFFICER

Fingers of R. 'V' hand flex as tips are drawn across back of L. wrist.

POOR, RUBBISH, SHODDY

Edge of R. little finger makes small anticlockwise circles on L. palm (also *awful, horrible, rotten*). Face/body show negative expression.

POSITIVE, PLUS

Extended index fingers form a cross, contact repeated for **positive**.

POST OFFICE, BANK

R. fist stamps heel, then fingers of L. hand. Single contact gives **bank**, and one version of **dole, endorse/ment, passport, benefit.**

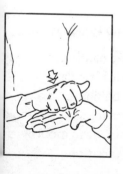

PREFER, PREFERENCE

Knuckles of R. closed hand, thumb extended, tap L. palm twice (also means **acceptable, good enough**), or side of thumb taps chin twice. May vary.

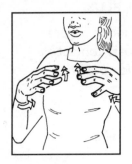

PREPARE, ALREADY, READY

Thumb tips of palm down open hands (one hand may be used), brush upwards on chest, twice, or tap twice against chest.

PRIEST, CLERGY, VICAR

'C' hands pull apart round neck in outline shape of clerical collar. One hand may be used, also a regional sign for *Preston*.

PRIVATE, IN CONFIDENCE

Edge of flat hand taps mouth twice, or flat hands, R. behind L., make small alternate side to side movements, near mouth, or other variation.

PROGRAMME (TV), FILM

Heel of R. open hand rests on L. index and makes small side to side shaking movements. Both hands may move down throughout.

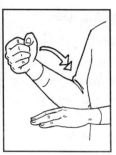

PUB, PUBLIC HOUSE, BAR

R. fist pulls back/down twice above left forearm held across body, (or R. hand only). Can be edge of R. full 'C' on L. palm, or moving to mouth.

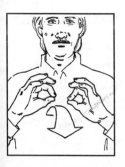

PUT OFF, DEFER, DELAY

Palm facing 'O' hands move in forward arc (also *postpone*). Hands move in backward arc towards body, for *bring forward* (in time).

QUALIFICATION/S

Hands in fingerspelt 'Q' formation make short movement down. Also means *qualify, qualified.*

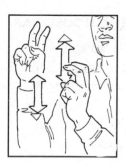

QUARREL, ARGUE

Bent 'V' hands, palms facing, move up and down alternately, twice, or same movement with indexes pointing towards each other (also *conflict*).

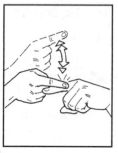

QUICK, BE QUICK, EARLY

R. index bounces sharply up off L index, or can be quick, repeated contact (*fast, hurry up*). Also means *emergency, sudden, urgent*.

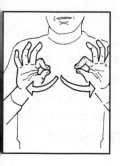

QUIET, BE QUIET, PEACE

Tips of 'O' hands touch, then move down/apart (may start crossed). May start with index on lips pressed together, or with 'Sh' lip-pattern.

RAILWAY, STATION, TRAIN

Closed hand, palm back/left, makes small repeated forward circular movements. Single firm forward movement gives *go by train*.

RAIN, RAINING, DOWNPOUR

Open hands move simultaneously down several times. Puffed cheeks and firm movement down/left give *heavy rain, downpour*.

READ, SCAN

R. 'V' hand moves across L. palm, or in manner to suit context (fingers represent eye gaze), or flat hands palm up/back (**book**) move side to side near face.

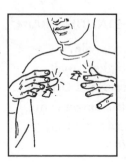

READY, PREPARED

Thumbs of palm down open hands (or one hand), tap upper chest twice, (can be upward brushing movements). Also means **already**.

REAL/LY, SURE, TRUE

Blade of R. flat hand hits L. palm, repeated for **actually, really, surely, truly**, or tip of R. extended thumb twists into L. palm (**real, really** regional).

REASON, BECAUSE

Edge of R. index taps left shoulder, twice. With appropriate expression for question form, also means *why?*

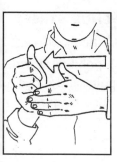

REGULAR, ALWAYS, USUAL

R. closed hand, thumb up, brushes along L. palm. R. hand can also be palm down, or palm back on L. Also means *habitual, ordinary.*

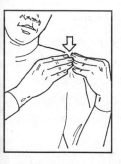

RESPONSIBLE, DUTY

Tips of bent hands move down to contact left shoulder ('N' hands may be used). Hands may overlap. Also means *burden, depend, rely.*

107

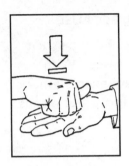

RIGHT, CORRECT, PROPER

R. closed hand, thumb out, hits L. palm. May contact chest (*I'm right*), or move and face forward (*you're right*), and so on.

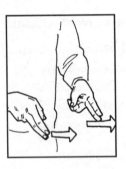

ROAD, AVENUE, STREET

Palm facing 'N' hands (or flat hands), pointing down, twist to point and move forward. Also means *method, path, style, system, way.*

ROOM, STUDIO

Indexes point down, (or sometimes point up), and move apart, and then back, in outline shape, or flat hands move in outline shape.

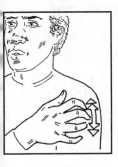

RUDE, BAD MANNERED

Tips of R. clawed hand rub up and down, twice on left upper arm (or on side of upper chest). Also means *impolite, impudent.*

SAD, DEPRESS, FEEL DOWN

Index edge of R. flat hand moves downwards on chest, or in front of nose, palm left (*serious, solemn*) or other variation. Mouth and shoulders droop.

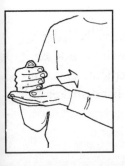

SAFE/TY, RESCUE, SECURE

Blade of R. bent hand on L. palm; hands move back to signer, or R. hand moves back across L. palm. Also means *salvage, save, protect.*

109

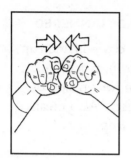

SAME, SIMILAR, TOO

Indexes extended, pointing forward, tap together twice (can be single contact), or R. 'N' hand touches nose, then palm up L. 'N' hand (regional).

SCARE, AFRAID, FEAR

Tips of clawed hand tap chest twice, body moves back. Body moves forward with raised brows for *really? surprised* (mouth turns down).

SCHOOL

Palm forward 'N' hand moves down in side to side movement, or palm back flat hand shakes side to side near mouth, or other variation.

SCOTLAND, SCOTTISH

Elbow moves in and out at side of body.

SHOP, SHOPPING

R. 'Y' hand rubs side to side on L. palm (also means *New York*), or palm down bent hands make small downward movement. Regional.

SHOW, DEMONSTRATE

Palm back flat hands held below eyes, move forward, down and apart. Also means *display, exhibit, exhibition, expose, prove.*

111

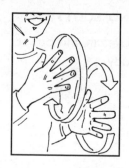

SIGN, SIGN LANGUAGE

Open hands move in alternate forward circles (may rub together), or twist forwards and back sharply (*chat*), or other changes in context.

SISTER

Edge of bent index taps nose twice. Bent index on nose flicks straight, or hand makes small downward twist for two regional variations.

SLOW/LY, AGES, LONG

R. flat hand (or index finger) moves slowly up left forearm, or palm down open hand waves downwards twice (*slowly, slow down*).

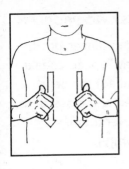

SMART, DRESSY, SUIT

Thumb tips move down chest. 'Y' hands can be used, or extended fingers of 'N' hand tap side of nose twice (*smart, posh*).

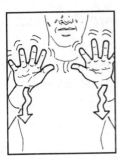

SNOW, SNOWFALL

Fingers of open hands wiggle as hands move slowly down with small wavy movements, or cupped hands press together (*snow, snowball*).

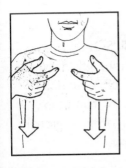

SOCIAL WORKER, WELFARE

Tips of palm back 'C' hands move down upper chest (also *missioner* now rarely used). May repeat. Fingerspelt abbreviation 'SW' also used.

SOFT, EASY, NO PROBLEM

Tip of index finger prods cheek (may repeat, cheeks may be puffed), or bent hands open and close onto thumbs several times (*soft, spongy*).

SOMEONE, ANYONE, WHO?

Index pointing up makes small horizontal circles. Large horizontal circle gives **everyone**. Face/body indicate if question form.

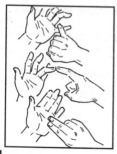

SON

Fingerspell 'SON', or R. index pointing left moves left across chin, or tips of palm back 'N' hand tap chin, or or other regional sign for **boy**.

SPEECH, SPEAK, SPOKEN

Fingers of 'N' (or 'V') hand open and close onto thumb in short forward movements, or index makes small forward circles near mouth.

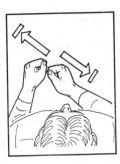

SPORT/S, ATHLETICS

Closed hands pull apart diagonally, twisting R. to palm up, L. to palm down, or indexes twist sharply forward from mouth or other regional variations.

START, BEGIN, COMMENCE

R. extended thumb brushes sharply down behind L. hand, or palm down open hands snap shut, twisting sharply to palm forward.

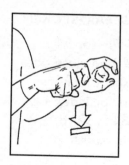

STAY, BE STILL, REMAIN

Palm down 'C' hands make small firm movement down (can be one hand), or bent indexes linked together move firmly down (also **stick, stuck**).

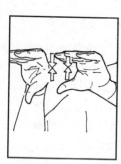

STOP, END, FINISH

Fingers of palm forward bent hands close onto thumbs (can be one hand), or palm forward flat hand held up, or other variations in context.

STRAIGHT, DIRECT, SOBER

Index edge of R. palm left flat hand touches nose, then hand moves and bends forward from the wrist. Will vary in context.

STRANGE, FUNNY, ODD

R. index flexed on thumb flicks out, moving sharply left in front of chin (also *peculiar, weird, stranger*). Nose is wrinkled. May vary.

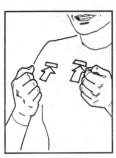

STRONG, ENERGY, POWER

Fists make short firm movement backwards, bending from elbows, or R. index moves in forward arc down left upper arm (*muscle*).

STUPID, DAFT, IDIOT

Knuckles of closed hand tap forehead twice, or tap against the underside of palm down L. flat hand, or other variations.

SUBTITLES, CAPTIONS

Palm forward 'C' hands move apart twice, or palm back clawed hand move side to side with fingers wiggling, or other variations.

SUMMER, STRANGER

Index edge of bent hand touches chin, then forehead, or is drawn across forehead to the right (*heat, summer*). *Stranger* varies regionally.

SURE, HONEST/LY

Blade of R. flat hand hits L. palm with emphasis. Also means *certain, definite, positive, real, true*. Open mouth closes with movement.

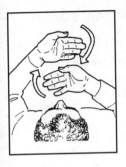

SWAP, EXCHANGE, SWITCH

Palm up flat hands change places, forward/back or side to side. Can be palm down 'O,' or clawed hands, or upright indexes (people), and so on to suit context.

SWEAR, BLAST, CURSE

Tip of extended little finger moves firmly forward from mouth. Lips may be pressed together, or form lip-pattern of various swear-words.

SWEET (taste)

Palm left R. index twists to palm back at side of mouth, or R. thumb tip moves across chin from left to right, or other variation.

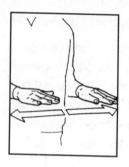

TABLE, ALTAR, BOARD

Palm down flat hands move apart. Also means *flat, ground, level, platform, slab*.

TAXI, CAB

Middle finger and thumb tip click together twice, hand held at head height. Often fingerspelt.

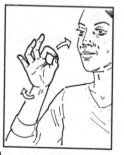

TEA, CUPPA

Palm left R. 'O' hand tips backwards near mouth, or same movement with closed hand, thumb tucked into bent index. Also means *cafe, cup*.

TEACH/ER, INSTRUCT/OR

Indexes contact sides of mouth, then make two short movements forward, down and apart. May vary.

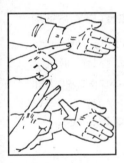

TELEVISION, TELLY, TV

Fingerspell 'TV', or indexes held together and pointing forward, move apart and down in outline shape (also *monitor, screen*).

THANK YOU, APPRECIATE

Tips of flat hand contact mouth, then move forward/down, or both hands move forward/down and apart. Also means *grateful, thank, thankful.*

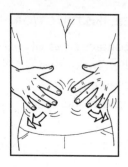

THAT'S ALL, ONLY

Palm back open hands shake downwards quickly twice, or palm forward open hands are held near shoulders. Shoulders are slightly raised.

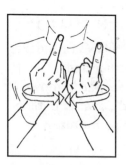

THING, ENTITY, ISSUE

Closed hands with indexes extended, twist slightly round and tap together twice. May tap repeatedly, moving to the right (*issues*).

THINK, THOUGHT

Index taps forehead. May make small circles (also *imagine, mull over, ponder, presume*) brows furrowed, or tap twice (*sensible*), brows raised.

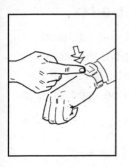

TIME, WHAT TIME?

R. index taps back of L. wrist twice, or fingers of open hand wiggle, or R. index on L. palm wiggles (also **clock**). Eyebrows raised if question.

TOILET

R. index of fingerspelt 'T' taps edge of L. hand (or palm) twice (also means **Tuesday**), or thumb of 'Y' hand brushes chest twice. Many variations.

TOMORROW, NEXT DAY

Index tip touches side of chin, then swings forward/down to finish palm up. With middle finger also extended, means **in two days time**.

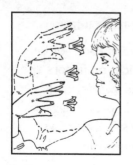

TRAFFIC LIGHTS

Palm back full 'O' hand springs open, moves down and repeats, twice. Both hands can be used simultaneously.

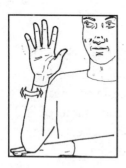

TREE

Right forearm held upright, resting on L. hand, R. open hand twists repeatedly from wrist. Formation moves round in arc for *forest, wood.*

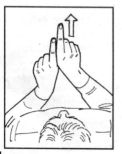

TRY, ATTEMPT, EFFORT

R. index brushes forward against L. Can be repeated. Single sharp movement gives *majority, most, mostly,* and *special, very* (regional).

TUBE, METRO, SUBWAY

R. index moves forward/left under L. slightly bent hand. Also means *tunnel, underground train, underground cable.*

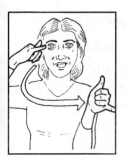

TYPETALK, RELAY CALL

R. 'Y' hand moves from side of head in forward arc towards L. 'Y' hand held forward. May vary. **TYPETALK** is a national relay service for text-phone users.

UNDERSTAND, IDEA, REALISE

Index finger flexed on thumb flicks up at side of forehead. Also means *initiative, invent, invention* (the eyebrows are raised). May vary.

125

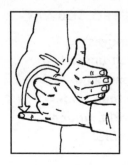

UNTIL, FINALLY

R. flat hand moves forward from left shoulder onto L. little finger (also **weekend**), or from right shoulder, to contact palm back L. flat hand.

UPSET, DISTRESSED

Flat hand makes two small upward brushing movements on chest. A single slow downward movement gives **calm, gentle, mild, quiet**.

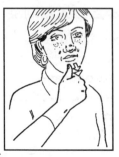

USE, USEFUL

Thumb brushes twice down chin, (or can be tips of bent hand). Index tip on cheek moves forward/down as hand springs open for **used to, au fait**.

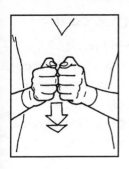

VALUE, VALUABLE, WORTH

Closed hands held together make repeated downward movement. Bunched hands can be used. Also means *precious*.

VARIETY, RANGE, VARIOUS

Indexes move up and down alternately as hands move apart, or with both moving right. Also means *assorted, etc, kinds, sorts, varied. Varies.*

VIDEO, VCR, RECORDER

Palm down 'V' hands make horizontal circles. Palm up open hands drop down closing to bunched hands for *video copy, record, taped.*

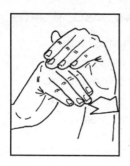

VISIT, ENTER, GO IN

R. bent hand moves forward under L., or faces and moves back to signer (directional). Can be 'V' hand prodding side of neck or other variation.

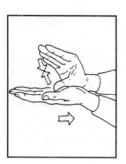

WAGES, PAY, SALARY

Fingers of bent hand close ono thumb, on L. palm, as hands move back to body. R. hand may be clawed and close as hands move back.

WAIT, HANG ON

Palm down bent hands (or closed hands) move down slightly, twice, or flat hand held up. As shown, is also a regional sign for *shop, shopping, London.*

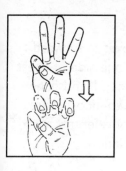

WALES, WELSH

Index, middle and ring fingers extended and open, palm forward; hand makes small movement down as fingers bend.

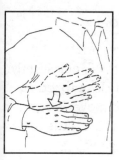

WANT, NEED, WISH

Flat hand makes small movement down on side of body, twisting to palm down. Also one version of *desire, hope*.

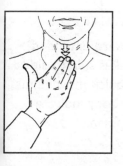

WATER, THIRSTY

Tips of bent hand brush down throat, twice, or thumb tip of 'Y' hand, or 'O' hand brush forward twice on cheek or other variations.

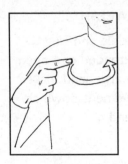

WE, US

Index moves in forward arc from one side of chest to the other. Handshape may vary to incorporate number of referents, or other variation.

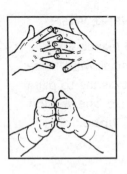

WEEKEND

Hands form brief fingerspelt 'W', pull slightly apart, and close together, or R. hand moves down left arm onto L. little finger. Regional.

WHAT? WHAT FOR?

Palm forward extended index shakes side to side in short quick movements. Face and body indicate question form.

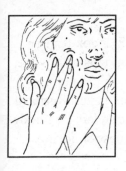

WHEN? WHAT TIME?

Fingertips of open hand wiggle against side of cheek repeatedly. Face and body indicate question form.

WHERE? WHEREABOUTS?

Palm up open hands (or one hand) make small inward circular movements, or move in/out towards each other. Face/body indicate question form.

WHICH? EITHER, BETWEEN

'Y' hand moves side to side or between items or people referred to. Directional. Face and body indicate if question form.

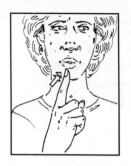

WHO?

Palm left R. index (can be bent index) taps chin twice, or thumb of 'L' hand on chin, index flexes. Regional. Lips are rounded, face/body indicate question form.

WILL, WOULD, SHALL, AFTER

Palm forward closed hand twists to palm down on side of cheek. Can be same movement with tip of exended index on cheek.

WIN, SUCCEED, ACHIEVE

Palm left R. clawed hand brushes sharply left across L. palm and closes to a fist. Can be R. hand only at head height, or other variation.

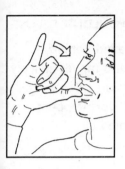

WINE

Palm left R. 'Y' hand tips backwards near mouth. Held straight with small tapping of thumb on chir means *pipe, smoke a pipe.*

WITH, TOGETHER

Index, middle finger and thumb of L. hand close onto fingers of R. 'N' hand. Formation may move forward (*go with, accompany*).

WOMAN

Side of index finger brushes forwards twice on cheek in small movements (also *feminine, girl*, and *always* (regional). May vary.

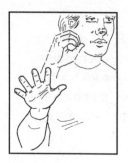

WON'T, WOULDN'T, REFUSE

Fingers flexed behind thumb; hand moves sharply forward from side of chin as fingers spring open, accompanied by headshake.

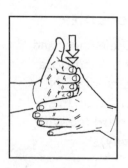

WORK, JOB, CAREER

Blade of R. flat hand chops down twice on index edge of L. flat hand, at right angles. Small sawing action gives regional sign for *wood.*

WRONG, EVIL, FAULT, SIN

Edge of R. little finger taps L. palm twice (raised brows for *what's wrong?*). May start with tips of open hand on chin. Can be R. hand only directed forward (*you're wrong*) or on chest (*I'm wrong*).

YEAR

R. index moves down to form fingerspelt 'Y' formation, may make single downward brushing movement.

YES

Closed hand twists to palm down, can be repeated nodding movement, may rest across L. index. Can be palm back (directional). Head nods.

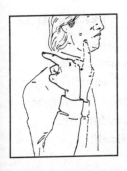

YESTERDAY, DAY BEFORE

Palm back index on side of chin drops down/back, or moves to point back over shoulder. Middle finger also extended gives **two days ago etc.**

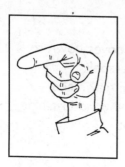

YOU

Extended index makes short movement forward or towards person concerned. Hand sweeps round in small horizontal arc for plural.

YOUR, HER, HIS, ITS

Palm forward closed hand makes short movement forward, or towards person concerned accompanied by eyegaze (also *your/her own* etc).

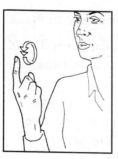

YOURSELF, PERSONAL/LY

Palm back index makes small forward circles directed towards referent, accompanied by eyegaze. Also means *herself, himself, itself.*

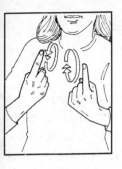

YOURSELVES, THEMSELVES

Palm back indexes make repeated alternate forward circles directed towards referents, accompanied by eyegaze.

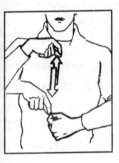

ZIP, ZIPPER

Tips of index and thumbs of both hands touch, then R. hand moves up and down. Location and direction can be varied according to referent in context.

APPENDICES

FINGERSPELLING

Fingerspelling is a manual representation of the letters of the alphabet, and although it is an important and integrated part of BSL it relies on the understanding of English (not the first language of most born deaf people) and its use varies considerably between individuals.

Drawings give a static image of the alphabet, but in fluent use, the shapes can merge and appear quite different, so that they are recognised as word patterns, and this requires practice. Words can be spelt out in full, abbreviated or initialised.

Fingerspelling is commonly used for names and places. Days of the week and months of the year are also often a repeated initial or abbreviated pattern,e.g. **Wednesday** - 'WW', **January** - 'JAN', and so on.

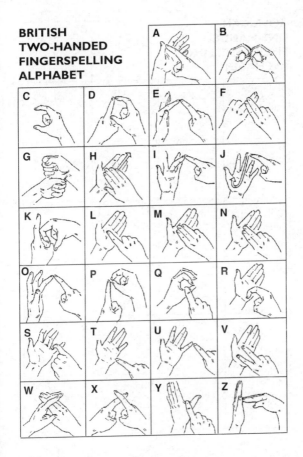

BRITISH TWO-HANDED FINGERSPELLING ALPHABET

AMERICAN ONE-HANDED FINGERSPELLING ALPHABET

		A	B
C	D	E	F
G	H	I	J
K	L	M	N
O	P	Q	R
S	T	U	V
W	X	Y	Z

SOURCES AND RECOMMENDED READING

British Deaf Association (1992). *Dictionary of British Sign Language/English*. London: Faber and Faber. ISBN 0-571-14346-6.

Pinker, S. (1994). *The Language Instinct*. London: Penguin Books Ltd. ISBN 0-14-017529-6.

Smith, C. (1990). *Signs Make Sense: A Guide to British Sign Language*. London: Souvenir Press. ISBN 0-285-65083-1.

Smith, C. (1992). *Sign In Sight: A Step into the Deaf World*. London: Souvenir Press. ISBN 0-285-65100-5.

Smith, C. (1996). *Sign Language Companion: A Handbook of British Signs*. London: Souvenir Press. ISBN 0-285-63333-3

These books can be obtained through local libraries, bookshops and the **Forest Bookshop** Mailorder Services, details and address in **USEFUL ADDRESSES** overleaf.

USEFUL ADDRESSES

British Deaf Association
1-3 Worship Street, London EC2A 2AB.
Tel: 0171 588 3520 (Voice) 0171 588 3529 (Text)
Fax: 0171 588 3527

Centre for Deaf Studies
University of Bristol, 22 Berkeley Square, Bristol,
Avon BS8 1HP. Tel: 0117 928 7080 (Voice)
0117 925 1370 (Text) Fax: 0117 925 7875

**Council for the Advancement of
Communication with Deaf People**
Pelaw House, School of Education, University of
Durham, Durham DH1 1TA.
Tel: 0191 374 3607 (Voice and Text)
0191 374 7864 (Text Ansaphone)
Fax: 0191 374 3605

The National Deaf Children's Society
National Office 15 Dufferin Street, London EC1Y 8PD
Tel: 0171 250 0123 (Voice and Text)
Parent's Helpline 2pm-5pm 0800 252380
Fax: 0171 251 5020

The Royal National Institute for Deaf People
19-23 Featherstone Street, London EC1Y 8SL.
Tel: 0171 296 8000 (Voice)
0171 296 8001 (Text) Fax: 0171 296 8199

The Forest Bookshop
(Books on Deafness and Deaf Issues)
8 St John Street, Coleford, Gloucestershire GL16 8AR.
Tel: 01594 833858 (Voice and Text)
Fax: 01594 833446
e-mail:deafbooks@forestbk.demon.co.uk.

LASER: The **La**nguage of **S**ign used as an
Educational **R**esource
c/o 8 Church Lane, Kimpton, Hitchen,
Hertfordshire SG4 8RP.
Tel:01438 832676 (Voice and Text)
Fax: 01438 833699
e-mail:laser@adept@nildram.co.uk.

Deaf Studies Research Unit
University of Durham,
Department of Sociology and Social Policy,
Elvet Riverside 2, New Elvet, Durham DH1 3JT.
Tel: 0191 374 2304 (Voice)
0191 374 2314/2306 (Text) Fax: 0191 374 4743
e-mail:BJClarke@durham.ac.uk.

TYPETALK: National Telephone Relay Service.
Pauline Ashley House, Ravenside Retail Park, Speke,
Liverpool L24 8QB.
Tel: 0151 494 1000 General enquiries.
Freephone 0800 500888 Registration (Text only)